SPRING

— A —
TIME
— TO —
GROW

*M*EDITATIONS

Anne Christian Buchanan

A
JANET
THOMA
BOOK

Thomas Nelson Publishers
NASHVILLE

Written permission must be secured from the publisher to use or reproduce any part of this book, except for brief quotations in critical reviews or articles.

Published in Nashville, Tennessee, by Janet Thoma Books, a division of Thomas Nelson Publishers, Inc., and distributed in Canada by Word Communications, Ltd., Richmond, British Columbia, and in the United Kingdom by Word (UK), Ltd., Milton Keynes, England.

Library of Congress Cataloging-in-Publications Data

Buchanan, Anne Christian.
   Spring : a time to grow / Anne Christian Buchanan.
      p. cm.
  ISBN 0-8407-9277-8
  1. Christian life—1960-   2. Spring—Religious aspects—Christianity—Meditations. I. Title.
  BV4501.2.B818   1994
  248.4—dc20   93–24552
                                             CIP

Printed in the United States of America
1 2 3 4 5 — 97 96 95 94

. . . .

To everything there is a season,
  A time for every purpose under heaven:
  A time to be born,
    And a time to die;
  A time to plant,
    And a time to pluck what is planted;
  A time to kill,
    And a time to heal;
  A time to break down,
    And a time to build up;
  A time to weep,
    And a time to laugh;
  A time to mourn,
    And a time to dance;
  A time to cast away stones,
    And a time to gather stones;
  A time to embrace,
    And a time to refrain from embracing;
  A time to gain,
    And a time to lose;
  A time to keep,
    And a time to throw away;
  A time to tear,
    And a time to sew;
  A time to keep silence,
    And a time to speak;
  A time to love,
    And a time to hate;
  A time of war,
    And a time of peace.

Ecclesiastes 3:1–8

. . . .

To Mabel Hendrix Purvis,
the most balanced person I know;
and to the memory of Ella Josephine Vause Christian,
who taught me about dewdrops and tulips

· ·

To Everything There Is a Season

The seasons of life are more than spring, summer, fall, and winter. There is a season when you prepare for childbirth and a season for saying goodbye to a loved one. There is the season of working hard for financial security, and there is the season of smelling roses and walking hand in hand with the one you love.

A season is not defined as much by an increment of time or the changing landscape as it is by a lesson learned or wisdom gained. And with each new season you will need a new set of skills and strengths. You will need endurance to face childbirth and understanding to help you grieve a loss. Patience and determination will be essential as you climb the corporate ladder, and peace and joy will accompany you as you walk with your partner through all the fields of life.

The *Seasons of Life Meditations* were created to be a friend traveling with you as you experience the joys and sorrows of each season. They will console, energize, counsel, chide, and inspire. These meditations contain the gentle wisdom of those who have experienced many seasons of

· ·

their own. While they may not completely understand your situation, the authors have been somewhere similar and can offer advice to help you understand yourself, your emotions, God, and your world.

The authors and editors wish you peace, wisdom, and love as you face all of your *Seasons of Life*.

*When April with its gentle showers
has pierced the March drought to the
root and bathed every plant in the
moisture . . . when . . . small birds
sing melodiously, so touched in their
hearts by nature that they sleep all
night with open eyes—then folks
long to go on pilgrimages.*
—Geoffrey Chaucer

*W*inter's over. (Well, almost.) Sun's out
(when it's not pouring rain). Air is warmer. Grass
is turning green. Birds are getting busy. And I
feel the urge to get busy too—to build something, grow something, clean something, make
something, or just to get outside and move.

This stirring, no doubt, is biological, the result
of being cooped up for too long. It's partially a
primitive physiological response to longer days
and more sunlight. But I think it's also a divine
nudge—an impulse from my Creator to be about
the business I was put on earth for.

And there's the rub, because I'm not always
certain what that business is! Spring has given
me the gift of renewed energy and a spurt of new
hope, but I'm not clear what to do next. Maybe
that's why my gardens often get planned but not
plowed, my exercise programs don't last, my

spring cleaning gets interrupted and goes unfinished.

Maybe before I fling open the door and run outside, I need to spend some time inside . . . inside me. Before I get busy with whatever projects offer themselves, maybe I need to go on an inner pilgrimage, to spend some time in journaling and prayer, to meditate on purpose and direction. I need to ask. . .

 My God, you gave me this restlessness, this urge to get busy. Grant me the purpose to know what I need to do with it and the courage and commitment to follow through even when this surge of energy ebbs.

*Love lives again, that with the dead
has been:
Love is come again like wheat that
springeth green.*
—John Macleod Campbell Crum

There's something about pain that just freezes a person up. When we've been hurt, when we've lost something or somebody we loved, we tend to tighten up, to shut down emotionally.

And this is not necessarily bad. Human protective mechanisms exist for a purpose. Psychologists tell us that depression is a normal and necessary response to loss; it's the body's way of slowing life down so that thoughts and feelings have time to adjust.

Just as winter allows the earth time to rest and prepare for new growth, emotional withdrawal can buy time for a wounded self to heal. But we can't stay frozen forever. We have to let ourselves thaw out.

A spring thaw can be gradual and gentle, the slow unfolding of a blossoming soul. Or it can be sudden and violent, like ice floes snapping and spring thunderstorms roaring. But with the thaw, sudden or gentle, comes release and the promise of greener days ahead.

I need emotional defenses. But eventually I also need the grace and courage to let them go.

*They considered keeping the soil
constantly stirred about the roots
of growing things the secret of
success. . . . The process was called
"tickling." "Tickle up old Mother
Earth and make her bear!" they
would shout to each other across
the plots.*

—*Flora Thompson*

'm no gardener. My thumb has not a tinge
of green. In fact, I routinely murder the plants
my daughter brings home from school; those
hopeful little sprouts in their egg-carton planters
just don't have a chance. The idea of grubbing
around outside in the dirt brings to my mind not
romantic, earthy images but hot, itchy, sweaty
ones. As a city girl raised by city folks, I'm pretty
vague about what one even does with a hoe.

But while I've basically come to terms with being horticulturally challenged, I wonder if I'm
missing one of the key messages of spring.

I've always seen springtime as play time, a
time to leave cabin-fever winter behind and to
run in the wildflowers. Spring fever always sets
up a tug of war between revelry and responsibility. But to a gardener, spring is a time for action
and for investment, a time to get started on the

work that will bring a summer bounty. And the gardener gets to play at the same time—to dig in the dirt and enjoy the sunshine and look forward to the future.

I also envy gardeners' clear connection between their work and its outcome. Too often I drive to the store and then go to the track to walk. Too often I neglect my family so I can work to support them. Too often I sit at my desk to do my work but never meet the people it affects. But in gardening the connection between work and purpose is clear: you break the soil, you pull the weeds, you harvest the tomatoes or the zinnias. I find that refreshing . . . and instructive.

Dear God, teach me the secret of integrating work and play and purpose—and show me how to invest it all for the purpose of growth.

> *He has put eternity in their hearts,*
> *except no one can find out the work*
> *that God has done from the*
> *beginning to end.*
>
> *—Ecclesiastes 3:11*

*I*n Texas, where I grew up, spring starts early—daffodils on Valentine's day, bright fields of bluebonnets in March, irises before April, roses before May. So I was fascinated when I first visited New England in June to see gardens full of irises and to hear that they had just finished with the daffodils. Back in Texas, lawns were already browning, and nature was already hunkering down under a hot summer sun!

That was the first time I really understood that not everybody's springtime happens at the same time. And that's not just true of the weather; that's the way people grow.

Most of us these days know about the various stages of human development. We expect to go through periods of separation and rebellion, growth and productivity, confusion and searching, certainty and contentment. But although it's helpful to know what to expect about the seasons of our lives, I think it can be dangerous to get too specific.

Every person is unique, with an individual set of body rhythms, past experiences, present circumstances. Individual responses and decisions shape the direction of our lives. Each of us experiences the seasons of life a little differently. And if we forget that, we easily fall into the trap of either comparing ourselves to others or judging them. Perhaps we can even bring on certain crises by anticipating them—as if it's "time" for an adolescent to rebel or a middle-aged executive to feel unfulfilled.

There's nothing wrong with being prepared for life's predictable crises. But we're not in charge of life's timetable. Springtime doesn't come at the same time for everyone—and that's true of summer, fall, and winter as well.

It's not our job to map out our lives—or anybody else's. It is our job to try to steer through each season with grace and integrity.

But I'm not dead yet . . .
—*British humorist*

*I*f you've never lived with small children or received a balloon bouquet, you may not be aware that helium balloons have a half-life. They come home from birthday parties and other celebrations all plump and hopeful, bobbing energetically at the end of their strings. A few days later they're at half-mast—not buoyant but not yet deflated. If they're made of Mylar, like the ones my husband received for his birthday, they can go on indefinitely.

So after a couple of dozen birthdays, I've finally come to terms with the necessity of balloon murder. It's hard, even painful, to plunge scissors or a needle into one of those bright bubbles. But if I didn't take matters in hand, our lives would be continually haunted by the ghosts of birthdays past.

And this skill of balloon murder has not been a bad one for me to learn because I'm one of those people who have trouble letting go of a good thing. I resist throwing things away, ending involvements, saying *enough*. At times I've held on to people and places and relationships and jobs long after they stopped having a legitimate place in my life. Even though I know I need to clear the ground before anything new can grow, I often cling tenaciously to the status quo.

Not everybody has this particular problem. Some people seem to have a special knack for saying "the end." These people may even need to learn to be less ruthless and more patient. But I believe I'm put on this earth to learn what *I* have to learn—and in my case balloon murder is a helpful lesson.

Lord, you go on forever, but not everything in my life has to! Grant me the wisdom to know when my "balloons" have seen their day. And remind me that if I stick with you, balloons will never be in short supply.

*Now to Him who is able to do
exceedingly abundantly above all
that we ask or think . . . to Him
be glory.*

—*Ephesians 3:20–21*

*M*agazine articles and pop psychology
books are always cautioning me about my expectations. Apparently many of my problems
(and everybody else's problems) result from unrealistic, unexamined expectations.

Do I expect to be rescued by Prince Charming? I'd better think again.

Do I expect approval for what I do and what I
am? I'd better find another source of self-esteem.

Do I expect people to read my mind? I'd better learn to communicate my wants and needs.

Do I expect life to be fair or even happy? I'd
better get real!

And all this is helpful to a point. But after
awhile I start wondering exactly what I *can* expect. Something deep within me rebels at the
cynicism of the apparent message: "Expect nothing; that way you won't be disappointed."

So what *can* I reasonably expect from my life
and my relationships? As far as I can tell, these
are the basics:

- In this world, I can expect to have problems—sickness, rejection, tragedy, interrupted plans.
- I can expect God to be with me through it all. I can count on God's comfort and God's strength if I can remember to keep turning to him.
- I can expect that eventually, over the long term, things will work out for the best. Not necessarily the way I planned. Not necessarily in ways I can see at the time. Not necessarily even in my lifetime. But I can reasonably expect that God will remain in charge and will continue to be good and loving.
- I can expect to be surprised with even more than I ever thought to expect—more than I could ever ask for or think about—if I keep myself focused on God's purposes.

Exactly how this all works is a mystery—I can't expect to understand it all. But I can trust you, Lord, to be with me as I learn to adjust my expectations.

Loneliness is the secret we keep from ourselves as well as from others.
—*Elizabeth O'Connor*

*T*he question was *In what social circles or times of your life have you felt "out of it"—like a stranger in a strange land?*

And the answer from almost everyone in the room was *I feel that way right now.*

"Since I graduated from college, I've had trouble finding women friends my age."

"I've lived in this town three years, and I don't have a single friend I can call on the spur of the moment and go out with."

"We rent in an upper-middle-class neighborhood, but we just don't have the money or time to live like our neighbors."

"I can't relate to the people I work with, and after work and dinner and time with my family, there's no time left to meet anybody else."

These were all normal, well-adjusted, productive people. All had families, jobs, activities. And all were surprised to realize just how painfully isolated and out of place they felt—at least part of the time!

Loneliness is epidemic in our cities and towns, in our workplaces, and in our churches and PTAs. It's partly because we move around so much, partly because we're so busy, partly because we're wary of strangers. Partly because it's human nature to drift into isolation unless we take specific steps to stop the drift.

I don't have the answers to this problem. I'm lonely too. But that night, in a circle of strangers, I saw connections being made. We admitted our loneliness to each other and to ourselves, and we sowed seeds of friendship and community. It was a good first step.

Lord, help me to tell the secret of my loneliness and then to look beyond it to the loneliness of others. Help me keep in mind that relationships aren't a luxury—and help me to make time in my life for the development and nurture of friendships.

Those who sow in tears
shall reap in joy.

—*Psalm* 126:5

A man on our street when I was growing up took all the grass out of his front yard and replaced it with gravel. He had a heart condition and wasn't supposed to do yard work. I can understand that. Besides, rock gardens look great.

But the strange thing was that this man insisted on *green* gravel. And he was the crankiest neighbor of all about keeping kids off his "lawn." Although he skipped the work of sodding and fertilizing and mowing, it seemed he still wanted to convince himself and others that he was growing grass. Of course, he wasn't fooling anybody. And he still had to do the work of defending his turf.

I think I sometimes do something similar with my own growth. I've done a lot of reading about spiritual growth and emotional healing. I'm familiar with what it means to be healthy. But much of the time, instead of investing in self-examination and real change, I put out some green gravel and *act* as though I've changed. Instead of working through my anger, I act mature. Instead of revealing my inner self to others, I act honest. Instead of tackling my selfishness and self-absorption, I act unselfish. Instead of "listening to my life" (to borrow Frederick Buechner's phrase) and learning from it, I pick up nuggets of wisdom from books and pass them on to others.

Like the man with the green gravel, I skip the effort and try to pretend the results are real. And I'm even better than he is at fooling other people and myself. But unless I give up on the masquerade of growth, I'm not going to do much real growing at all. It's hard for grass to grow underneath all those rocks!

Lord, teach me to invest honest pain to achieve honest growth.

> *What we anticipate seldom occurs;*
> *what we least expected generally*
> *happens.*
>
> —Benjamin Disraeli

*M*y daughter learned in kindergarten that March 21 is the first day of spring. So she appeared in the kitchen that morning in shorts and a tank top, despite the fact that it was thirty-five degrees out and the biggest blizzard of the century had dumped eighteen inches of snow on us a week earlier. In her mind it didn't matter what the weather was like. It was *supposed* to be spring.

I do the same thing. Oh, I can usually pick out clothing that's appropriate for the weather. But I base so many of my feelings and reactions and decisions on what I think is supposed to be instead of responding to the way things really are. And too often those assumptions are as faulty as assuming a calendar day determines the weather—especially in March!

Why do I keep thinking I can really pull an "all nighter" to finish a deadline the way I did fifteen years ago? The reality is I'm older. I have more family responsibilities. I have other deadlines pending, so I can't spend all my energies on one big push.

And why do I keep picking fights with my husband because he sleeps late and I have to get up? The reality is I married a night owl who does his best work at one in the morning and whose work doesn't require him to get up early.

And why do I keep acting as if life is going to be fair, as if people are going to appreciate me the way I think they ought to, as if I will be able to tackle my problems and weaknesses without help? I know better, but somehow I keep expecting the universe to fall in line with my ideas of what ought to happen.

It's really kind of arrogant. More to the point, it's really self-destructive.

I get a lot more done when I give up on what is supposed to be and pay more attention to what is.

*I say only half-jokingly . . . that
when the time comes for me to die, I
will not have time to fit it into my
schedule.*

—*Andrew Greeley*[1]

It's the flu, all right. My head feels like an oversized ball of papier-mâché. My body feels like it's just gone nine rounds with Leon Spinks *and* Rocky Balboa. I lie on the bed staring stupidly into space. Then I think I'm feeling better, so I get up and attempt to type a sentence or wash a dish. The world reels—back to bed. But inside I'm wailing, "I don't have *time* for this . . ."

I don't think anybody lives a full life anymore; everybody I know lives a *packed* life. There's no white space on the calendar. We have to schedule time for rest and play and even sex—if we don't, it doesn't happen. And something unexpected, like the flu, can bring the whole structure crashing down.

And we're not talking about frivolous activities. Most people I know have long ago pared away the nonessentials and are down to the basics: work, family, nutrition, hygiene, and an occasional sanity preserver such as a movie or a softball game.

I don't have the final answers to this ongoing dilemma, but my flu experience did give me a few insights I hope I can hang on to when the fever's gone:

- If my happiness is dependent on getting everything done, I'm going to be miserable for a good portion of my life. I've got to go elsewhere for my self-worth and for my sense of fulfillment.
- If my schedule can't survive a bout with the flu, maybe something's wrong with my schedule.
- This overload has to do with where I am in my life and with commitments that bring me joy as well as stress. There may be a time later when the nest is empty, my job has wound down, and my commitments are few. So maybe I need to thank God for my heavy schedule even as I try to find ways to adjust it.

Dear Lord, I ask you for healing—both of my body and of my life-style. Thank you that you have blessed my life with people to love and work to do. Teach me gratitude . . . and help me find sanity.

*He has made everything beautiful
in its time.*

—*Ecclesiastes 3:11*

The big oak entertainment center was my father's most ambitious project to date. A self-taught woodworker, he had put together an end table, a credenza, and other odds and ends of furniture. But this built-in cabinet, intended to house his stereo and his record collection, was much larger and more complex than any of these—and he was designing it himself.

I remember watching as that unit slowly grew to become part of our living room. First there was the clutter of rolled-up plans, then sawed boards leaning in the corner, then a long cabinet and shelves sprouting above it. For awhile, sawdust was everywhere; then the stink of varnish permeated the house. Finally the cabinet was finished, and it was magnificent—one of a kind.

What I remember most clearly, though, is that through the whole process, Dad kept messing up. He had never built a piece like that before, so mistakes were inevitable. A measurement would be off, a piece wouldn't fit, a great idea would prove impractical. And whenever that happened, Dad simply redrew his plans. He incorporated the mistake into the original design and continued building around it.

I think that's the way that most of us grow. Our lives take shape bit by bit with frequent mistakes and miscalculations, often with some inconvenience and irritation for everyone involved.

The difference, of course, is that we—the works in progress—are the ones messing up. But amazingly, our Designer still knows what he's doing, even if we don't. If we let him, he can work around our mistakes and miscalculations and build them into the plan—working and reworking to shape us into something both beautiful and unique.

Lord, half the time I don't know what I'm doing with my life—even when I think I do. Thank you for being creative and persistent and loving enough to redeem my mistakes and make me beautiful.

> *If a thing is worth doing, it is worth doing badly.*
> —G. K. Chesterton

$\mathcal{I}$ was raised to appreciate fine music, but one of my favorite singers couldn't carry a tune in a bucket. He was a high-school friend, a gifted young man who excelled in art and English, earned straight As, and presided over many organizations. Music was not his strong suit; he had trouble singing two consecutive notes in the same key. But he loved to sing! And I loved singing with him, because his enjoyment was so infectious. He taught me the truth of Chesterton's statement that anything worth doing is worth doing badly.

That does not mean there should be no standards or that we should do less than our best in any given area. Shoddy or lazy work is an insult to our Creator and a betrayal of the gifts he put in us. The act of doing something well can also bring great satisfaction and pleasure.

But I sometimes wonder if our contemporary emphasis on excellence is robbing us of the joy of doing things just for fun—not to mention preventing the growth that comes with trying something new. Many of us, if we aren't talented or skilled in a particular pursuit, tend to hang back from learning or even trying it.

It takes courage to do something badly and enjoy it—to dare to sing off-key, to produce clumsy paintings, or to stretch our uncoordinated muscles to play softball. But the benefits, I've discovered, are wonderful. It's hard to take myself too seriously when I know I'm not a genius—and that knowledge also makes me more tolerant of others' less-than-perfect efforts. But the chief benefit, I believe, is the built-in joy of using my eyes, using my muscles, using my voice—not because I'm good at it, but because it's worth doing!

Anything worth doing is worth doing badly—and all things are worth doing joyfully.

*He will rejoice over you with
gladness,
He will quiet you in His love.*
—*Zephaniah 3:17*

When I was nine, my dad was in graduate school, and we lived in campus housing for married students. That meant concrete floors, grungy walls, wall-to-wall beds, a torn Naugahyde sofa, and no pets. But there was a big field next door where we could run and catch bugs. There was a swing set in back under a big sweet gum tree; we could swing really high and kick the sweet gum balls. And just around the corner was my forsythia playhouse.

The bush had grown large in a circular pattern spreading long, willowlike branches out from its trunk until they touched the ground a foot or so away. This created a kind of tunnel around the trunk. I could crawl in from behind and be completely out of sight behind the curtain of branches.

It was a great place to hide, to read, to play, to daydream. In winter, it was dry and crackly and protected from the wind. In summer, it was cool and green, soaked in leafy shadow. But early spring was best, when the whole bush was covered in bright yellow flowers. Even the light inside my playhouse was yellow.

It's one of my most exotic memories—spending an afternoon in a little room made up entirely of golden blooms. Sitting there made me feel both safe and excited, free but protected—and incredibly privileged. I mean, most of my friends had more stuff than I did, but *nobody* had a playhouse made out of flowers!

Remembering that special place gives me a beautiful picture of what it means to be surrounded by God's love. I seem to spend much of my life in grungy surroundings doing what needs to be done. Whenever the grayness pulls me down, I need to stop, close my eyes and see myself as I really am—God's child, tucked safely inside his care, incredibly privileged, and utterly surrounded by beautiful, golden light.

Dear God, thank you . . . thank you . . . thank you for loving me so much. Help me remember that, in your love, I'm still a lucky little girl.

Spring is sprung; the grass is riz—
I wonder where them flowers is?
                                        —Old rhyme

*W*e planted beans in a little cup, watered them, and put them in a warm window to wait. Five minutes later she was leaning on the windowsill, disappointed that nothing was happening. And although I smiled at her vague concept of time, I knew how she felt.

I have spent a lot of my life in the time warp between planting and sprouting, between making my move and seeing results, between doing what I could and knowing whether I did the right thing. I apply for the job, but I won't hear yea or nay for days or even weeks. I invite a new acquaintance to lunch, not knowing whether friendship will flower. I have the biopsy, but they'll call me in a few days with the results. I work on a committee, teach a class, or pray for someone, but only time will tell whether my efforts have made a difference.

Whether it's filled with excited anticipation or fearful dread, waiting is hard. And it's especially hard when I realize that I may not see results even in my lifetime.

Something deep inside me clamors for closure.

Like my three year old, I don't *want* to wait and see how the future unfolds; I want to know now! But life usually doesn't work that way. Much of the time, I'm stuck with waiting. But while I wait, maybe there are some things I need to ask myself:

- Have I really done all I can do—including pray?
- Is there something I need to learn while I'm waiting—about patience, trust, or overcontrol?
- Are there matters I need to attend to in the meantime? Is my frustration distracting me from other matters that need my attention?
- Do I need a perspective adjustment? Have I fallen into the child's trap of thinking the only reality is what happens *now*?

 Lord, Psalm 90 reminds me that "a thousand years in Your sight Are like yesterday when it is past." Give me the gift of your perspective whenever I feel caught in a time warp.

> *Imagination [is] . . . Reason in her*
> *most exalted mood.*
> —*William Wordsworth*

*M*y six-year-old daughter is a spinner of tales. She loves to dream up fantasies and tell them to me. She also embellishes her factual reports. A simple report about what happened at school will gradually evolve into a delightful piece of fiction replete with unicorns.

And that poses a dilemma for me. I believe in nurturing imagination. I'm convinced we learn to solve problems in our lives by coming up with ideas that depart from what we've always done and thought. And I love my daughter's stories. Her imagination brings me delight. But I also believe in honesty, in speaking the truth to myself and others. Without honesty, our creativity is of little help in solving problems, because problems have to be faced before they can be solved.

This isn't a problem for children only. Do you ever struggle to find a balance between what is and what might be? Do you ever wonder at what point a positive attitude becomes denial or when rigorous honesty becomes hard-edged fatalism? For me, it's easy to tip the balance—to live in a dream world or to get trapped in the cynical realism of thinking things will never change.

I think the key to balance here is to realize that imagination and realism aren't the polar opposites we make them out to be. Surely honesty must recognize the power of dreams, and the best imaginative tales hold a clear mirror to truth. Imagination is best used in a way that opens up reality, not runs from it.

To help us both find that balance, my daughter and I have set up a practice of calling a "reality check" *after* the story. She's free to embellish her tales at will, but I'm also free to call for a more down-to-earth account when I need it. It's too early to know if this practice will help us keep in touch with what is without losing heart for what might be, but it shows promise.

Dear Lord, teach me to nurture the gift of imagination without losing touch with your truth.

*Coming down the hill it is delightful,
cool, and pleasant. The sweet
suspicion of spring strengthens,
deepens, and grows more sweet
every day.*

—*Francis Kilvert*

It's only March, and already the magazines
are pushing the panic button: swimsuit season is
around the corner. Better start that diet, better
get serious about your situps, better start check-
ing out the various brands of tan-in-a-bottle.

In just a few months, they all promise, I can
drop ten pounds, tone up, shape up, and find a
swimsuit that will flatter my particular figure
type. All I have to do is look past the chocolate
cake recipes and follow their brand new, quick-
shape-up plan.

But I've heard all this before, and this year I'm
not buying it. Yes, I want to be trim and toned (it
will take more than ten pounds). I would also like
to be strong and organized and balanced. But
I've grown leery of three-month solutions to life-
long challenges, and I refuse to spend my spring
fixated on summer.

This has nothing to do with whether I have
winter flab to lose. I do! But I am convinced that
positive growth is not a once-and-for-all, get-it-

done-and-get-it-over-with proposition. Growth is not a brief campaign that ends in a season of triumph. What happens *after* swimsuit season?

As I see it, growth is a daily tending in a positive direction—the kind of growth that "strengthens, deepens, and grows more sweet every day." I may need a plan to guide my decisions. And I may have—*will* have—some setbacks along the way. But I will continue making progress as I concentrate on the small, day-to-day decisions that take me the direction I want to go. In the meantime, if I keep my attitude adjusted, I'll have the added bonus of enjoying the journey.

I'm in my life for the long haul, not for swimsuit season. I will make decisions that move me toward sweet, steady growth.

> *Rise up, my love, my fair one,*
> *And come away.*
> *For lo, the winter is past,*
> *The rain is over and gone.*
> *The flowers appear on the earth;*
> *The time of singing has come.*
> —Song of Solomon 2:10–12

*I*t's dogwood season here in East Tennessee. Unfortunately, it's also tax season.

Today as I drove to my accountant's office with my bulging folder of receipts, the hills beside the roadway were gorgeous. Dogwoods draped the brown and green hills with elegant drifts of white. Redbuds bloomed pink. The sun was smiling to apologize for weeks of drizzle. And I was on my way to spend another couple of hours contemplating dismal financial realities.

It seems to happen every year. I spend an entire April angry and depressed because I just don't have time for spring. I've got tax stuff to do and job stuff to do, commitments to honor and promises to keep. And this year is especially bad. Sickness and bad weather and a string of other calamities have thrown me impossibly behind.

But I hate to have spring happen without me. Neglecting to celebrate, failing to savor the beauty seems somehow shortsighted. Restricting my revelry to a passing appreciation on the way to an appointment just seems wrong.

There are long-term solutions to my April dilemma; I know that. I need to plan better, organize better, prune my commitments, limit my promises. And I really want to do better—next year. But in the meantime I've booked a cabin in a nearby national park for part of the weekend. I've marked it on my calendar—in ink. My little girl and I have serious plans to ramble in the woods.

Getting away will cost me a lot of late-night hours in weeks to come. But I'm determined not to hole up in my house, my office, or my accountant's office, and let another dogwood spring drift by me.

Sometimes joy is a discipline and celebration is a responsibility.

When it rains it pours.

—Old saying

*F*irst it was the flu, the kind that really knocks you out. Then came the snow—eighteen inches that paralyzed this Southern town for almost a week. Then my computer blew up—not literally, but it felt that way. And I need my computer to make a living.

That was March. Next, April brought "financial disaster week." We lost the renters in the house we can't sell. The house was vandalized. A banking mistake sent checks bouncing. Then we got the verdict on our income tax. *Gulp.*

Sometimes life seems to happen like that—a raging spring flood of calamities and inconveniences. Growth takes a back seat to survival; we do what we have to do to get by. And I don't have any real wisdom to offer in this situation; I'm right in the middle of it right now. But here are the principles I'm clinging to like tree branches over white water while I wait for things to calm down. *(Help!)*

- *Lay off the blame,* of others and of myself. People are only human, and sometimes things just *happen.*
- *Don't get isolated.* Problems can build walls be-

tween people. I need to ask for help and offer it.

- *Give myself a break*. I can't expect to recover
  from weeks of disaster in just a few days. And
  all I can do is all I can do.
- *Avoid paralysis*. I can't do everything, but that
  doesn't mean I should do nothing. I can take
  steps to handle the most pressing matters.
- *Take care of myself*. Developing an ulcer or sink-
  ing into depression won't help matters, but
  adequate exercise, rest, and nutrition might.
- *Take joy breaks*. I need to take time to notice and
  celebrate the things that are going right.
- *Remember that life won't always be like this*. Please,
  God, say it won't!

*It's a cliché, but "this too shall
pass." My task is to hang on
and keep growing!*

*If you are walking on the Decatur
Road when winter turns spring, you
will probably slip and fall and hurt
yourself. It is a mud-happy stretch
at this turn, and if you are not
careful you could very well slide
all the way into Decatur.*

—Joe Coomer

The old-time preachers called it *backsliding*.
And that's exactly how it feels when you've
made significant progress, really grown in some
area, only to fall back into your old habits.

You've stuck to your eating and exercise plan,
and your faithfulness has been rewarded by
toned muscles and a smaller dress size. Then one
day you're a slug in front of the TV, mainlining
ice cream again.

You've disciplined yourself to handle each
piece of paper only once, filing papers away or
tossing them as they hit your desk. And you've
reveled in the sense of order—until one day you
put aside a paper to "think about it," and before
you know it you're shuffling through a haystack
of correspondence just to find an eraser.

It's an irritating and discouraging experience,
but it doesn't have to send you all the way back
to the mud puddle any more than a cold snap

after Easter has to signal a new ice age. You always have the choice to stop your slide by reaching for help and changing your direction. And the old-time preachers had a word for that too—*repentance*.

Don't let any "holy roller" connotations get you down here. *Repent* isn't a browbeating term; it's a promise of hope. It means that with God's help, no matter how far back you've sloshed, you can climb out of the puddle and move forward again.

It's not easy. You have to face what has happened, face your own weakness, confess it to God and to others, and ask for help. It may take awhile to climb back up to where you were. But what a relief to have the chance to do it!

Lord, give me the insight to look behind the old clichés to discover truth—and hope.

So he looked, and behold, the bush was burning with fire, but the bush was not consumed. . . . So when the LORD saw that he turned aside to look, God called to him from the midst of the bush.

—*Exodus 3:2, 4*

It was just a little Bradford pear tree, the kind they use where I live for landscaping commercial areas. With its thin, straight trunk and its round ball of branches and leaves, it looked a lot like a tree in a child's drawing. With its three sisters, it occupied a little island in the shopping center parking lot.

My four-year-old and I were headed to the Fresh Market to grab a dose of comfort. After only six months in the city, a thousand miles away from most of my friends and family, I felt keenly the emptiness of being a stranger. I could walk all over town, and no one would recognize my face.

We got out of the car and started over to the little store whose fresh flowers, free coffee, and bakery fragrances usually made me feel welcome. And then my daughter noticed it: "Mommy, look, the tree is singing."

I stopped to look and then broke out in a

smile. It was true! Evidently a flock of songbirds on their way north had decided on a layover in that parking lot. But they were all nestled deep beneath the leaves. All we saw was the pretty little tree almost quivering with their music.

It was a magical moment. The two of us stood holding hands for a long moment, listening. My daughter was entranced. And I was overcome with gratitude. For to me, the message of that tree was, "No matter where you go, you won't be a stranger to me. I'll always be here to give you even more than you thought you needed."

You see, I was looking for comfort that day. But God sent me magic!

Lord, if you can speak through a burning bush, I guess a singing tree isn't that much of a challenge. Give me eyes to see you and ears to hear you speak.

The excessiveness of life is the best
sacrament we could ask for, a hint
of how powerful, how determined,
and how excessive You are.
                              —Andrew Greeley

*M*y part of the world is really going all
out on spring this year. Explosions of dogwoods
and redbud. Fields blanketed in wildflowers.
Lawns breaking out in an impossible, eye-
popping green. Even the bird's song is exuberant
and unrestrained—*Tweet!*

In a way, I expect spring to be energetic and
excessive. It seems normal. So if I don't take time
to listen, I might lose the message: there's nothing
inherently wrong with excess, and there's a time
in life for going all out.

I need to hear that message especially right
now, at my particular (middle-aged) time of life.
Like many people, I was an extremist when I
was young—pouring myself into my loves and
my enthusiasms with seemingly endless energy.
But as I matured, I had to back off. I realized
there are limits to my time and my energy; I
learned to assess my resources realistically and
reserve my "big guns" for the most important
battles.

The trouble is, sometimes I've gotten that message wrong. Instead of choosing my battles, I've ended up putting my guns in cold storage. At times I'm in danger of becoming too careful with myself and my energies—not reaching out, not taking risks, not investing myself fully in anything. It's easy to mistake meanness for moderation, stinginess for self-discipline, laziness for maturity, fear for wisdom.

And that's why I've got to get into my head the message of a burgeoning spring. God is a God of abundance, even a God of excess. He doesn't do things halfway. And while he wants me to grow up and learn wisdom, I don't think he means for me to back off from risk. There really are times to go all out.

 God, only in your love can I learn the balance of choosing wisely but investing myself fully. Teach me the gift of excessiveness when it comes to faith, hope, love, and joy.

> *Stones and trees speak slowly and
> may take a week to get out a single
> sentence, and there are few men,
> unfortunately, with the patience to
> wait for an oak to finish a thought.*
> —Garrison Keillor

*A*cceleration seems to be the key word for this time in the late twentieth century. Everything seems to be moving faster and faster—cultural changes, unfolding events, the exchange of information, the onrush of birthdays.

To keep up, like most of my friends, I've perfected the act of doing many different things at once. I listen to tapes while I drive. I swab out the sink while I'm waiting for the water to get hot. I straighten my desk while waiting for a client to call and listen to the news while I cut up onions for dinner and talk to my daughter about school.

My days are measured, judged, by the ticking of the clock and the flap of a desk calendar. And I suspect that, most of the time, the din of passing time and the unspoken verdict of "not enough" drowns out the voice of God in my life.

It's not that God can't use the rushing events to communicate truth to me. It's just that trying to keep up with the clock and calendar does something to my hearing. I don't know if it's a secret of the universe, but so far it seems to be true in my life. If I want to remain spiritually alive, connected to the Reality that transcends time, I have to consciously slow down, jump off the time wagon. And that's not easy. I can set aside a quiet time, even make reservations for a silent weekend, and at first I'm left twitching, still ticking, unable to settle into the slow rhythm of the earth around me.

Only gradually am I learning that slowing down is not something I can "fit into" my tight schedule. That's missing the point. What I need to do is block out the hours, if necessary, and then let myself settle in, slow down, until I feel myself fitting into God's schedule. Breathe deeply. Relax with music, journaling, stretching exercises—whatever it takes. Read something that will assist the connection—meditative literature, thoughtful essays, Scripture. Or just sit and let my mind slowly settle.

And gradually the ticking and the twitching will calm down, and in the silence I may hear his voice.

Slow time is never wasted time if I spend it listening.

Rain, rain, go away . . .
                              —*Nursery rhyme*

*I*t's one of those weeks when everybody seems depressed. Rain has been drizzling and pouring for five days straight (too many April showers). Bad news is all over the TV: a slumping economy, a virus going around, too much work for everybody. The convenience store clerk is frowning and distracted. The doctor's receptionist is irritable. My daughter is impossible. And I long to talk to someone who's openly, sincerely upbeat.

Some days it really does seem as if someone has thrown a wet blanket over the whole world. Whether it's one person's attitude or some sort of general malaise, times like that are murder to get through.

So how do we get through them? To a certain extent, of course, we need to just grit our teeth and hang on. Chances are the rain will eventually stop, people will get well, the economy will swing the other way, our hormone level will change.

But things don't always get better. Floods, depressions, wars, and epidemics really happen. Relationships sour. People turn on each other. Institutions fall apart. So I'm wary of depending

. . . .

too much on "the sun will come out tomorrow."
Probably it will. But what if it doesn't?

I think Jesus had a much more realistic and
workable approach: "In the world you *will* have
tribulation," he warned, "but be of good cheer, I
have overcome the world" (John 16:33). If we
depend entirely on the world around us to bring
us happiness and fulfillment, we'll be at the
mercy of gray days and sour circumstances and
the cataclysms of history. If we keep our focus on
a deeper reality, we'll be able to see the rays of
hope that keep shining even on the grayest days.

*God, you said there would be days
like this! You also made it clear I
don't have to be at their mercy.
Teach me to know you, to lean on
you, to focus on your light within
me. (Meanwhile, if it fits your plan,
how about some sunshine?)*

. . . .

And God said, "See I have given you . . . everything that creeps on the earth, in which there is life, I have given every green herb for food." . . . Then God saw everything that He had made, and indeed it was very good.

— *Genesis 1:29–31*

The little commuter flight took me home over a spring patchwork of blooming orchards, greening meadows, new-plowed fields—a patchwork of pink and green and brown. Delighted by its beauty, I was suddenly reminded of our wedding-ring quilt.

My husband's grandmother made it before she died—years before he and I even met. She pieced it pink and green, like the spring landscape, stitched it in patterns as elaborate and orderly as the farms and houses below me, gave it to my husband's mother with strict orders that it be given to him on his wedding day.

And she left instructions, a handwritten note whose dour sternness is softened by the obvious love invested in the gift.

"This quilt is to be used as a comfort to your body," she ordered, "not to be trampled under

. . . .

your feet. Use it with thanks and obey God always."

I am sure she was thinking of all the lovingly stitched quilts that have ended up as moving pads, dog beds, car blankets. When I was growing up (before quilts became a valuable commodity), every family seemed to have a collection of torn old quilts that they used for a multitude of humble uses. That wasn't the fate Mama Ginny had in mind for this creation.

Now, as I see the earth-quilt spread beneath me, I muse that it was given to us with the same kind of love and the same kind of warning. The earth was given to us for our enjoyment, for our comfort, to clothe and feed us and give us joy. But implicit in the gift are the instructions that we use it and not abuse it, that we remember always the painstaking love that went into its creation, and that we always give thanks.

Lord, you have given me this earth to walk on, but never to trample under my feet. Teach me to live on this planet with care and with gratitude.

. . . .

*Seek first his kingdom . . . and all
these things will be given to you
as well.*

—Matthew 6:33 NIV

I have always been attracted by the idea of a
stripped-down life. Something in me resonates to
the idea of getting rid of the extraneous and getting down to essentials. Part of my spirit longs
for the clear-eyed focus of the uncluttered sur-
face, the bare cabin, the cleared schedule, the single rose. Yet I live among a clutter of
knick-knacks, bookshelves, paper piles, and
back-to-back appointments. I moved from a
three-bedroom house to a tiny apartment and
kept most of the furniture. My walls are full. My
desk is full. My life is full.

Why do I have so much trouble eliminating
and concentrating? Part of my problem involves
a reluctance to make hard decisions, to choose
one road and leave another behind. But I also
think it comes from the fact that the things and
people and activities that junk up my life also
bring me some comfort and security. Somewhere
deep is the terrified question *If I get rid of all the
clutter, will there be anything left?*

What that tells me, of course, that I'm in need
of deep-down healing—healing at the trust level.

Somehow I need to believe that simplicity doesn't mean sterility or emptiness—that even if I'm stripped down to my bare skin, God is still God, and God still loves me.

Maybe that's the whole point of my yearning for simplicity. It's a yearning for reassurance that there's a meaning, a relationship, a Person at the stripped-down core of my life. Once I've gotten that message, then everything else can be given to me as well.

God, you created a universe of astonishing complexity and detail. But until I trust that you are there at the core of my life, all the details will simply cause me stress. Teach me to focus on you first, then to live in simplicity, abundance, and trust.

Gold and crimson tulips, lift your
bright heads up.
Catch the shiny dewdrops in each
dainty cup.
If the birdies see you as they're
passing by,
They will think the sunset dropped
from out the sky.
—Song my grandmother taught me

The snapshot is one of our family treasures.
One wrinkled, ninety-two-year-old face, with a
few wispy white hairs escaping from under the
knitted cap. One round, rosy, two-year-old face
framed in golden curls. There they are, forehead
to forehead, both grinning in delight.

It had begun as a painful visit. My grandmother had been declining visibly every time I
saw her. Wheelchair bound, she seemed increas-
ingly weaker, more out of touch, sometimes lost
in her own inaccessible world.

Still, we wheeled her out into the courtyard so
she could enjoy the breeze. We introduced my
daughter, who was curious but a little frightened
by the strange, shriveled-up creature in the roll-
ing contraption. Then we just sat and chatted
while my daughter played, shyly circling closer
and closer.

· ·

And then—*connection!* Light sparked in the old woman's eyes; she smiled and leaned forward. The little girl grinned and came closer. They touched foreheads and smiled at each other, friends. Dad snapped the picture.

We couldn't have engineered that moment. But it couldn't have happened if we hadn't prepared for it—if we hadn't made the effort to visit, if we hadn't bothered to bring the baby, if we hadn't brought the camera.

When I was a very young girl, that same grandmother taught me a little song about tulips who lift up their heads and catch the dew. I've taught it to my daughter. And I'm grateful that at least one time we were ready, heads up, to catch a little bit of heaven in our lives.

God, I believe you send us moments like this to help us develop a taste for your love and your wonder. Teach me to live with eyes open and head up, open to the moments of your grace.

· ·

How can I be lonely? I'm the one in charge of celebrations!

—Byrd Baylor

It's festival time in East Tennessee (and every other place I've lived). Every little town, every ethnic group, every plant and crop seems to have its designated celebration. Through April and May, we've celebrated arts and crafts, dogwoods, azaleas, and ramps (sort of a wild onion); gardens in general and gardens in particular; Native American culture, Greek culture, English culture, Scottish culture, and Appalachian culture; two or three events of local history and three or four civil war battles; fiddle playing, gospel singing, and storytelling. If I wanted to, I could go to a party every weekend.

Part of the impetus behind the celebrations is economic. Festivals are public relations ventures, business lures, opportunities to sell to a specialized audience. And as far as I can see, they're all fundamentally alike. Every festival features food vendors, sound stages, silly contests, and souvenir tents. There are kids in strollers, Labs on leashes, young people in costumes, and racks of commemorative T-shirts.

But I'm convinced there's more going on here than fund-raising and "me-tooism." Surely these

· ·

festivals began as healthy responses to a deep, God-given impulse: spring's here, the world is beautiful, we're alive—let's get together and celebrate (and eat, and dance, and wear decorated T-shirts).

Writer Charlie Shedd once quoted a psychiatrist friend as saying that one indicator of emotional health is the ability to say "Yes," "No," and "Whoopee." Well, spring weekends were tailor-made for "Whoopee." Besides, what's wrong with having a party every weekend? Maybe I'll throw one myself!

God, your love is reason enough to celebrate. Today I have you—and springtime too. What can I say but "Whoopee?"

· ·

*Pray for one another, so that you
will be healed. The prayer of a good
person has a powerful effect.*
                              —James 5:16 TEV

*M*y husband and I don't fight often, but
this one was a doozy. We didn't throw lamps and
china; we didn't beat on each other or even
yell—that's not our style. But we dredged up old
hurts from the past. We butted our heads against
deep-seated differences that we can't or won't
change. We said things that were intended to
hurt, and they did.

Eventually, we both calmed down, and we
found some measure of reconciliation. We reaf-
firmed our commitment, even though we weren't
wild about each other at the moment. We kissed
and made up but went to sleep still troubled.

The next morning I ran into a friend. In the
course of our chatting, I told her about the fight.
And she said, "You know, I woke up in the middle of the night thinking about you guys, and I
said a prayer for you."

That offhand comment blew me away. Suddenly I was overwhelmed with a sense of being
watched over and cared for. And although that
crisis is long since over—my husband and I are

friends again—the memory of that prayer still warms me.

The idea of praying for people has always been a little problematic for me. I've been in religious circles where people say "I'll pray for you" in automatic response to trouble—sort of a religious version of "There, there." I may be cynical, but I don't always trust that "I'll pray for you" means anything. I don't know what your experience is; maybe "I'll pray for you" makes you even more nervous.

But I have to say that this prayer was real, and it was wonderful. To have someone think about me specifically and lovingly and offer me to God's care—what a wonderful gift! All I can say is *thank you*.

*Lord, I don't always understand
how prayer works, but I know you
live in us as we love and care
for each other. Grant me the
faithfulness and sensitivity
to pray for others as my
friend prayed for me.*

> *It's a truth we want to pass
> on to our children: Nobody's
> perfect—we're all jerks saved
> by grace.*
>
> —Kathy Peel

She's attractive, intelligent, creative, fair-minded, kindhearted, hardworking—altogether an exemplary human being.

She's ugly, stupid, selfish, bigoted, lazy, and petty—a blot in the annals of history.

And she's me. At least, she's how I think of me.

I once read that being able to hold two diametrically opposite views at the same time is a sign of intelligence. In this case, I think it's more a case of not wanting to face the real truth about who I am.

I mean, it's appealing to think of myself as good and talented. There's a kind of romantic satisfaction in thinking of myself as irredeemably wicked—a hopeless case. But to see myself as just another a flawed human being, someone who means well but cannot manage to get through life without messing up—well, that's just embarrassing.

And if I'm really honest, I have to admit that this is what the real me looks like. I am competent in some areas, gifted in a few. I care about people. I work very hard. And yet, again and again, I fail to do what I think is right. I hurt the people I care about—not necessarily out of wickedness, but out of selfishness or stubbornness or just plain carelessness.

This me is not a stellar human, not the chief of sinners, just sort of a jerk. And without some sort of outside intervention, this is the me I'm stuck with! I may be brilliant or determined or well-intentioned or all three. But I don't have what it takes, over the long haul, to escape from "jerkhood".

Thank heaven—literally—for the good news of God's amazing grace. If I let him, God has the power and the willingness to release me from both delusions of goodness and delusions of wickedness. As I depend on him, he will grow me into the specific, beloved person he created me to be—the real, real me.

Only by God's grace can I look at myself honestly and still live with what I see.

*Perfect love means to love the one
through whom one became unhappy.*
—Søren Kierkegaard

*T*hey've been married forty years this spring.
Overall, it's been a fruitful union—two kids,
three grandkids, a sizable contingent of friends
and colleagues, and a slate of satisfying accomplishments. Despite nagging worries about
health and kids and retirement, they're more or
less content—and proud of themselves for coming this far.

But the fight they had this week was the same
fight they've had off and on since the week after
their wedding.

She likes to talk.

He doesn't.

She gets her feelings hurt.

He feels pressured.

Both get irritated. Sparks fly.

Yes, they've each changed over the years. Circumstances have changed them. In some ways,
they've worked at changing. Certainly they've
adapted to each other and learned to work
through problems. But even now there are issues
they have never resolved. For the most part,
they've learned to just accept—but not always.

In a sense, it's a little depressing. Surely after

all those years, they would have put those problems to bed. But in another sense, they give me hope that it's possible to persist and forgive and keep hoping even when some issues resist resolution. They remind me that it's possible to live a satisfying, full life even with unsolved problems and unresolved conflicts.

How else can we flawed human beings hope to live together?

Lord, I need both discernment and commitment for my relationships to work. Help me to know where to push for resolution and where to accept our differences.

> *Casting all your care upon Him, for*
> *He cares for you.*
>
> —*1 Peter 5:7*

*A*h-ah-ah-chooooo! For me and for many others, spring is allergy season. Drifting pollen, new-mown grass, dust-stirring spring cleaning—all have the power to reduce me to a pitiful heap of sniffling protoplasm. Years of habit cause me to explain the multitude of symptoms as "just allergies." But this is not a piddling affliction. It takes my precious time. It saps my energy. It hampers my work and my relationships.

So why do I squirm at the idea that God is deeply concerned with me and my allergies? It's hard to shake the habit of thinking that God really doesn't want to be bothered with such petty miseries. Sure, he's God of the universe, God of the major crisis. But God of my hay fever? That seems a little strange. That's like saying he's God of my constant insecurity, God of my broken ice maker . . . even God of my hangnail!

Then novelist Andrew Greeley, in his remarkable prayer journal, gently reminds me that God's love is specific and personal and passionate—big enough for a world in pain but tender enough for a stuffy nose:

> While I was reading the psalm this morning—and sniffling and sneezing—I was momentarily taken by a sense of how much You love each of us. . . . You have a mother's love for the dope addict, the woman living on a machine for four years, the kid killed yesterday in a fight over a sports jacket . . . the mugger lying in wait for a victim, the overweight person hardly able to walk, the Iraqi soldier waiting in his trench. . . . You love each of us with a unique and special love. . . . You suffer when each of us suffers, an enormous amount of suffering. You are vulnerable and fragile with our vulnerability and fragility, a vast weakness. Only God could possibly stand it. . . .
>
> I believe in that love. Either You are that way or You are not and the second option is inconceivable. Help me to understand better Your love and live in the palm of Your hand.[1]

 Lord, I present my sneezing, wheezing, miserable self to you. I need you. Help me believe that you really do care.

The only way to get control is by giving up controlling. It's a paradox that's not easy to comprehend. But it is so.

—J. Keith Miller

*O*ut of control. Too much to do. I'm forgetting commitments, neglecting significant people and important tasks. I'm eating too much and exercising too little. That little voice inside is gasping, "Gotta get organized, gotta get in shape, gotta get moving . . ."

So naturally I take the action that is most appropriate—the one most likely to get me the results I want and need. I gripe at my husband, yell at my kid, and give unwanted advice to a friend!

Sometimes I think the most difficult task in life is learning what we can control and what we can't control—then acting appropriately. And I'm convinced that a large majority of our problems stem from getting confused about which is which.

That's true for me. When I feel unusually insecure, I end up tightening my grip on something I really can't control—like other people. I become critical, blaming, manipulative, or just extra "helpful." Then I either get slapped in the face for my efforts or I alienate the people I care about. And frustration rules because my efforts to control the uncontrollable are doomed to failure.

On the other hand, when I fail to take responsibility for what I *can* control—*my* attitude and *my* behavior and *my* spiritual commitment—life frays around the edges. Important matters slide. I let myself down, and I let others down. Self-confidence takes a nose dive.

I've been both places, overcontrolling and undercontrolling. Often I'm both places at the same time—flailing helplessly in my own bad habits while I try to eradicate someone else's, haunted by that inner refrain of "I gotta . . . I gotta." Either way, I lose out on becoming who I was meant to be.

Lord, you know what I really "gotta" do. I gotta learn to take responsibility for what's mine, not for what's none of my concern. And to do any of it, I gotta learn to lean on you.

April is indeed the cruelest month of the year—nature striving painfully to be reborn.

—Andrew Greeley

*T*t's the birth season, the season of new life. New sprouts show themselves in plowed and seeded fields. Chickies and bunnies and lambies arrive on the scene (and in the pet stores). I get visions of a Bambi spring, with birds singing and adorable little animals running to welcome each newborn addition. What a charming time for my pregnant friend to have her baby. Every little one should have an April birthday.

I'm thrilled to welcome all this burgeoning new life. But I've given birth before, and my friend's recent experience brings my own to mind. I rejoice at new birth, but I am acutely aware of how difficult and painful and messy a process it can be.

I'm not just talking about labor—although labor certainly has its moments! There's also the growing discomfort as the time approaches. (I remember a walking buddy, eight and a half months along, wishing she could just set her swollen stomach off to the side and rest for a few minutes.) There are inevitable worries and doubts that mingle with anticipation. *Will the baby* be healthy. *Will I be a good mother?* There's the hard work of getting everything ready, the anxiety about how you'll behave under pressure, the discomfort of recovering from this major event.

Yes, it *is* worth it, as most new mothers will tell you. But birth takes a lot out of you.

I need to remember all these difficulties whenever I'm involved in bringing new things to life. New goals, new callings, new careers are exciting, thrilling—fulfilling. But the actual process of getting them born is often painful and sometimes messy. In my experience, birthing new life calls for courage and endurance, not mushy sentiment. I will do well to remember that as I look forward to the exciting new experiences of my life.

Lord, you went through the agony of death to give us new life, so you know just how hard bringing in the new can be. Grant us the strength we need to do our part.

> *Fair daffodils, we weep to see*
> *You haste away so soon.*
> —*Robert Herrick*

Just a few weeks ago, the whole town seemed touched with magic. Trees bubbled with bloom. Parking lot dividers and corporate landscaping waved with tulips and irises. Vacant lots sported wildflower weeds. Even the slums were spruced up with flowers.

And now, so soon, the magic has faded. Floral confetti litters the ground around trees as branches shed their blossoms and get down to the business of being green. Parking lots are parking lots again. Vacant lots have been mowed. The slums have settled back into their everyday despair.

And it's a little sad, this fading of spring— almost like a little death in the middle of life. In such a short time the magic is set aside; life turns ordinary again.

Maybe it's an obvious metaphor, but the magic in our lives and our relationships fades too.

I remember times when romance bloomed along with the daffodils, when my newborn and I discovered together the wonder of a caterpillar and an acorn, when a new friendship unfolded in the sunshine of acceptance and shared confidence. And all that fresh loved changed, faded—either into the energetic, exhausting business of growing or the withering heat of conflict and boredom.

Some relationships shriveled. But some (thank God!) bore wonderful fruit. And that's the point, I guess.

Lord, the magic always fades. That seems to be the way you've made things. Teach me to savor the freshness of new love and new relationships but to let go of the magic with good grace and to put my energy into growing.

> *Do not lay up for yourselves*
> *treasures on earth, where moth*
> *and rust destroy and where thieves*
> *break in and steal; but lay up for*
> *yourselves treasures in heaven. . . .*
> *For where your treasure is, there*
> *your heart will be also.*
> —*Matthew 6:19–21*

*U*pkeep has never been my strong suit. I'm more inclined to the grand gesture, the creative sweep. I like building, organizing, whipping up from scratch, starting over. I'm less patient with tending, patching, cleaning, and putting away. My housekeeping tends to be of the "let it all pile up till it drives you crazy, then clean like mad" variety. As a worker, I tend toward the "put it off, then panic" approach.

But despite these haphazard tendencies—or perhaps because of them—I've learning to appreciate maintenance. I'm having to face the fact that I can't always muster a successful, last-minute effort, and I don't always have time for eleventh-hour cleanups. Regular upkeep allows me to take advantage of last-minute opportunities and saves me from the humiliation of being caught in disarray. If I don't grow in the discipline of maintenance, I risk becoming tired, bitter, and defeated. In a sense, maturity demands maintenance.

But even as I work to cultivate the habits of tending, patching, cleaning, and putting away, I've got to keep perspective on *what* I'm trying to maintain. It's possible to spend all my time and my energy maintaining and defending things that I am doomed to lose anyway—things like youth and health and material possessions and even life itself. Better to concentrate my maintenance efforts on items of eternal significance— my connection with God and my relationships with other people.

I need the disciplines of tending, patching, cleaning, and putting away. Even more, I need the disciplines of faith, hope, and love.

*We admitted we were powerless . . .
that our lives had become
unmanageable.*
—*Step One of the Twelve Steps
of Alcoholics Anonymous*

It's the one complaint guaranteed to raise my hackles: "But I can't . . ."

"I can't draw."

"I can't sing."

"I can't do math."

Whether it comes from adult or child, I bristle when I hear it. And I *hate* to have to say it! I was raised to be a "can do" kind of person. Deep down, I'm convinced I can do anything if I put my mind to it. Having to say "I can't" smells like failure to me. It feels humiliating.

And it *is* true that "I can't" easily becomes a self-fulfilling, self-limiting prophecy. (As my grandfather used to say, why would you want to prove yourself wrong?) I've seen people robbed of joy in whole categories of life because they told themselves "I can't." Sometimes "I can't" really means "I'm afraid to try," and it gets in the way of growth.

But I'm gradually learning (the hard way) that "can do" can be as damaging as "I can't." Maybe I really can do anything if I'm willing to make the tradeoffs. But the tradeoffs are significant, and in many cases the payoffs are just not worth it. I am a human being—subject to the limitations of talent and time and choices made. That means that in many situations, learning to say an honest "I can't" is not a form of self-sabotage but a necessary lesson in humility. If I persist in "can do" and fail to weigh the tradeoffs, I let people down, I end up feeling like a failure, and I pass up an opportunity to grow.

To rephrase the famous Serenity Prayer:

Lord, grant me the serenity to accept the things I can't . . . The courage to do the things I can . . . And the wisdom to know the difference.

*Let us eat and be merry; for this
my son was dead and is alive again;
he was lost and is found.*
—Luke 15:23–24

I don't know why I decided to look into that hole again, but I'm glad I did.

Our cat Freddie had escaped from our apartment, and three days later he was still missing. Now, this is not a tough, streetwise animal but an overweight, sheltered house cat. We couldn't imagine his fending for himself. So we worried— and searched. We called his name, put up posters, and checked at the Humane Society. Finally we gave up searching, although we still hoped he would find his own way home.

Then this morning I decided to check the little opening into the apartment-building basement one more time. And this time my call was answered with a faint meow. Within minutes I was reaching through that small opening, trying to hoist a fat (but hungry) feline four feet off the floor. Now he's sprawled as usual on the bed, all four legs in the air—and I can relax.

Okay, I know he's just a cat. But the experience of losing him and finding him helps me understand a little more personally the story that Jesus told about a father and his wayward son.

The son finally slunk home after wasting his whole inheritance and ruining his life. He knew his father would disown him—but the father just wanted to celebrate!

Jesus made it pretty clear that God is like that father. We can spend our lives running from him. But when we're ready to come home, he's eager to welcome us. For the first time, in a small way, I can vouch for that. Freddie put us through a lot of worry and work, and it was pretty stupid of him to run away. But when we found him, my only response was gladness. And that makes me feel a lot better about going home myself!

Dear Lord, you speak to me in little ways as well as large, and this week you've spoken to me through my cat. It's hard to believe you love me so much—but thank you.

> *God is an inveterate risk-taker.*
> —Elizabeth J. Canham

She's a sweet child, a pretty child, my daughter's best friend. And I'm a little embarrassed to admit this, but something about her gets on my nerves. It's not because she's loud or rude, but because she's so careful with herself.

When she was visiting the other day, we climbed the hill behind our apartments. I thought it would be fun to take the back way down—a little wooded path. The minute we started through the sparse underbrush, she started worrying that she would "put out an eye." Later on, we went to a playground. There, she worried about getting overheated. I have no fear of this child's being hit by a car; she won't even venture onto a parking lot. While she plays, she worries about snakes, poison ivy, and being abducted.

I have no idea why this child is so fearful. Perhaps she was sick a lot when she was younger; perhaps she has an overprotective parent. For me, however, the issue is not what her problem is but what *my* problem is. Why do I find this child so irritating? I'm afraid the answer is all too apparent: it's because she reminds me of me.

Some people are born risk takers; they love to live on the edge. In the interest of balance—and perhaps to remain alive until their next birthday—they may need to temper their daredevil tendencies.

But people like me and my daughter's friend have a different kind of challenge. By nature, we are prone to spend a lot of energy taking care of ourselves—anticipating trouble and avoiding it, steering clear of danger, avoiding risk. In the interest of growing, we need to learn to step out, to venture forth, to take a risk when a risk is called for—trusting that God will keep us safe.

 Lord, I know in my head that risking myself by depending on you is not really a gamble. Please hang in there with me while I gather up the courage to act on that knowledge.

*And lo, I am with you always, even
to the end of the age.*
—Matthew 28:20

*W*ant to see a teacher explode?

Just try making a remark about working "only" six hours a day—or "only" nine months a year. If you are not injured, you'll be quickly enlightened about what happens behind the scenes of the teaching profession—curriculum development, lesson preparation, conferences, grading, career development, and much more.

Of course, that is true of almost any pursuit; a large portion of the work goes on behind the scenes. Behind every corporate report lurk weeks of research, writing, and emptying the coffeepot in the middle of the night. Behind every speech hide hours of scribbling, editing, and even declaiming before the mirror. Behind every clean house kneels a householder with a vacuum cleaner and a bottle of all-purpose cleaner.

It's a mistake to assume that the only work that counts is work that is immediately visible. But I think I do that a lot with God. Either consciously or unconsciously, I evaluate God's work in my life according to whether I can see progress or feel his presence. If I can't, I often assume he's not on the job.

But there's so much about God's work I can't see—at least not until later. What feels like intense conflict may be his preparation for a new era in my life. What feels like spiritual dryness may be his strategy for drawing me closer to him. Ordinary events may actually be a series of sacred opportunities that I'm too dull to perceive. In other words, I often can't see what God is doing in my life—but that doesn't mean nothing's happening!

And I *know* all that—so why can't I remember it?

Father, grant me the perception to see your work in my life—and the faith to assume you're working even when I can't see it.

This is the day the LORD has made;
We will rejoice and be glad in it.
—Psalm 118:24

Spring's spectacular phase is over. Right now there are no cloudbursts or flash floods, no glorious, can't-stay-inside weather or breathtaking floral displays. I'm not in love—at least not at the moment. It's just an ordinary spring day—filled with ordinary activities, an ordinary husband and child, ordinary friends.

In a sense, this is the kind of day that most tries my faith, my hope, and my love. There's nothing like a good crisis to increase my energy and remind me how much I need God. There's nothing like a gorgeous day to remind me to rejoice. And there's nothing like a little romance to motivate me to be a better, more caring person. (It's even motivated me to lose weight!) But persevering through my everydays, learning to be loving and faithful and joyful day after ordinary day—now, there's a challenge!

But the Psalm tells me, "This is the day the LORD has made"—and I see no specific mention of crisis days or drop-dead-gorgeous days or days when my hormones and my heart are hopping. The Lord has made even this boring, slightly irritating day, and I am called to learn from it and to rejoice.

How? Maybe I can learn to rejoice in doing what is right even when I don't feel like it. Maybe I can learn to rejoice in subtle beauty—a sparrow's brown, mottled markings; a friend's quiet voice; the graceful pattern inside a cut onion. Maybe I can rejoice in love that takes a less gaudy form, love that shows itself as faithfulness, loyalty, and consideration. And maybe those things are more important to my growth than all the spectacular circumstances I'm motivated to rejoice about on nonordinary days.

Lord, you are God of the huge and the minuscule, the spectacular and the ordinary, the dramatic and the daily. Teach me to rejoice in every day that you have made.

> *For there is hope for a tree,*
> *If it is cut down, that it will sprout*
>   *again,*
> *And that its tender shoots will not*
>   *cease.*
>
> —*Job 14:7*

*C*an't be fixed: a child's face stares bleakly up at me over the plastic shards of a shattered toy.

Can't be fixed: the giant oak lies among the hurricanes debris, its roots upended helplessly.

Can't be fixed: the man and the woman stare across the distance between them, shocked into silence by brutal words finally uttered.

Some things in life can be patched up, shored up, repaired, or redone. But some wounds are too grievous, some blows too shattering, some rifts too wide to be pulled back together. Some experiences—a divorce, a betrayal, abuse, neglect—leave us permanently wounded, our psyches disfigured. We live, we go on, but we're not really *fixed.*

Yet I believe there is an alternate plan for things that can't be fixed. It won't work for shattered plastic, but this plan can make an astonishing difference in living, growing things like trees and people. I've seen it in a new shoot growing from a shattered stump, in the faces of a couple whose counseling sessions are finally showing some progress. I've seen it in people who have hit bottom and admitted their own helplessness, only to begin growing again from there.

As far as I can see, God's strategy for broken trees and limbs and lives and souls is not repair but growth, not being patched up but being granted the gift of starting over.

Can't be fixed—but can be reborn.

Can't be fixed—but can be made new.

Lord, the older I get, the more I feel like a patched-up collection of old wounds and badly healed scars. I give you my broken pieces. And I beg you not to fix me, but to make me new again.

> *How lucky we are to have such a
> treasure of memories.*
> —*Lady Byrd Johnson*

*I*t's not the official end of spring. Practically speaking, though, Memorial Day is the gateway to summer. School's out. Schedules change. People head for the beach and the ball field.

But many also head for the local cemetery or the Vietnam Memorial. For Memorial Day is intended to be more than the first three-day weekend of summer; it's a day for remembering. Today's paper is packed with interviews—men and women remember their wartime experiences, rejoicing in what was gained and mourning over what was lost and pondering the meaning of their experiences.

When I think of it, that's not a bad thing to do on a regular basis—to journey into memory for the purposes of understanding and instruction and perspective and gratitude.

That process has not been easy for a friend of mine who was sexually abused as a child. She has very few memories of her growing-up years. The protective mechanism that allowed her to survive also robbed her of so many important experiences. Only through extensive therapy has she been able to undertake a painstaking excavation of her memories—and uncovering those ugly and beautiful artifacts has helped her find peace and healing.

My dad has been writing his memoirs. Often, as he works he uncovers a forgotten bit of experience, a memory that teaches or delights him—and he is grateful to realize just how rich his life has been.

So today, I salute my own memories—happy and painful, good and bad. I celebrate past happiness for the joy it has woven into the fabric of my being. I acknowledge past pain for its lessons (some learned, some left behind) and for its gift of empathy. And I set aside this time to ask myself: Where have I been? Whom have I loved? What have I learned? What mistakes have I kept on making? Where has God's grace been working in my life?

Lord, as I take time to remember, show me what you have to teach me from the past. Teach me to be grateful for yesterday while moving into today.

> *God is great, and therefore He will
> be sought; He is good, and therefore
> He will be found.*
>
> —*Anonymous*

*A*s a person who sunburns under a full moon, I have never qualified as a sun worshiper. So now—in this era of sunscreen—I get a certain amount of satisfaction watching the in crowd hide from the rays. Even now, in spring, the articles start to appear, urging us to get prepared for "sun season."

According to the article I just read, protecting ourselves in these days of ozone depletion is a full-time occupation. We're supposed to put on high-octane sunscreen first thing in the morning and replenish it during the day because it is almost impossible to hide from the sun. Ordinary T-shirts won't keep out those UV rays. Hats and umbrellas don't keep out reflected sun. Only a good sunscreen, applied conscientiously, offers adequate protection from wrinkles and skin cancer and "horrid" age spots. Even with sunscreen, we're advised to stay indoors between the hours of eleven and three.

All of this sounds a little scary—and it's a lot of trouble. But if I turn the whole picture around a little, I get a vivid picture of how God's love works. We talk about seeking God, when in reality his love, like those UV rays, is always seeking us. He is positive, powerful energy that seeks me out and helps me grow (no horrid age spots here). His love surrounds me all the time, even when I can't see it. If it can't reach me directly, it will find me another way. There's only one way I can avoid its effects—by choosing to say no to it—and even that doesn't always work.

Lord, you surround me and seek me out even when I think I'm seeking you. I want to bask in your love and mercy.

It is possible to begin again, It is hard and we never do it perfectly, but it can be done.

—Andrew Greeley

I finally got the desk cleaned off, and I swore I would never let myself get in such a mess again. Now, as I peer through the mounds of paper, I realize I need to start all over again.

I worked hard to get in shape, and I swore I would never let myself get flabby again. Now, as I puff up the stairs, I know I need to start over with that, too.

I finally made room in my schedule for a desperately needed daily quiet time. And now, looking around with tired, panicked eyes, I realize that's gone down the tubes too. I need to start over once more.

Sometimes I get so tired of starting over. It's humiliating to face the fact that I've messed up yet another time, to go back to square one and try again. I start feeling like that old song about Michael Finnegan—where every verse ends with "begin again" and the whole song starts all over. After awhile, the repetition gets on your nerves!

But do I really think I'm going to get rid of my bad habits and self-destructive ways in one campaign, one organizational frenzy? Do I really think that one round of good intentions—or even thirty rounds of good intentions—will exempt me from making mistakes? And do I really think the only mistakes I'm allowed are the ones I've never made before?

If I understand anything at all about God, it's that his love and his grace are infinite. God is not concerned about the number of times I have to start over; God just wants me to keep growing and leaning on him. I don't have just three chances to get it right; I can begin again any number of times. Most of the time, it's my own shame and unrealistic expectations that hold me back.

For me, at least, trying again after I've failed repeatedly takes a tremendous amount of courage. It feels like a huge risk because the stakes are higher, so it requires a stronger dose of humility and grace. But maybe it can also bring me to a clearer understanding of who I am, who God is . . . and why I need God in the first place.

Okay, God, I'm ready if you are—let's try it one more time. Remind me that I can do it only with your help. And thank you for your gift of infinite new beginnings.

NOTES

1. Andrew Greeley, *Love Affair: A Prayer Journal* (New York: Crossroad, 1992), pp. 61–62.